DEEP WITHIN MY SOUL

A compilation of fourteen poems, thoughts, expressions and
feelings based on the many experiences in the life of a woman

By

Regina Jele-Ncube

D1583871

© 2015 Regina Jele-Ncube
ISBN: 978-1-910115-44-2

Cover design by Tasfia Tasneem
Prepared for Publication by LionheART Publishing House
Published by SeanLinus Books, UK

Dedication

For my mum, Lucy and my 'little sister', Patricia. Two
strong, sensitive women.

Acknowledgements

My love for poetry was re-ignited by a competition held in recognition of refugees in the UK. I met a very down-to-earth woman who loves people and encouraged me to enter the competition. Rona Grabowski, many thanks for being a part of making this dream a success.

As the path of life meandered and took twists and turns, I consider it a blessing to have met a very inspirational young man. I am indebted to Dumi Senda for his massive input to this project and for his friendship. They were times where I doubted and questioned if I should carry on, he encouraged and believed in me right to the end. Dumi, there is still more work to do, bro. You are a credit to mankind.

Lastly but not least, I would like to acknowledge and thank my two children Nonky and Kenny who are my world. I love you dearly guys.

Contents

He Communicates..1

The Mountain Cries..3

A Better Half of Humanity 5

Only I 9

Somehow 11

Woman 14

Mother... 16

Motherhood 19

Fruits of my Womb... 22

The Small Suitcase 25

Hope 28

Connecting Souls... 31

Give me my Flowers.. 35

Love Me... 38

About the Author: 41

About the Compilation 43

He Communicates

Many a time you speak and converse with me
In the quiet of the night, in the midst of a crowd
You still reach out.

I could be at work; you still reach out
If I had my way, at times I would run away and ignore you
But you never give up
You still reach out.

Why such an interest in me?
There is never a moment you are not reaching out
It could be words spoken through a brother or a sister
Still you reach out.

It could be through a song, a recited poem, watching children play
You reach out.
A sister that holds and hugs me when I am distressed
You still reach out

Teach me to listen
To hear your still small voice
Teach me to embrace the moments when you speak and reach
out
For somebody somewhere is struggling to hear you

Teach me to listen
To embrace those intimate moments with you
For someone is struggling to distinguish your voice
While you reach out and speak
I will listen.

Behind the Inspiration

Whether we are women of faith or no faith at all (having no faith is in itself faith) we all hear that small still voice that at the best of times we cannot work out. I have learnt to listen to that voice. It is the voice of reason.

The Mountain Cries

Dawn has broken, and the valley comes alive
The stately mountain overlooking the valley greets the morn
The valley gazes at the mountain stately standing
That mountain of refuge

As the valley shouts the morning song
The stately mountain echoes back
As though to warn him of her untold secrets
And the cry that haunts in the dead of the night

The road up the stately mountain; many a weary foot trod.
In quest to satisfy the curiosity of their souls,
And to celebrate the tranquil peace
Once offered by the mountain.
Her cries invoke memories of those that once scaled her.

Cries from the heaven-touching mountain deafens the ear,
And the valley is disturbed.
The majestic mountain has a secret of old.
The valley watches in desperate anticipation.
The mountain cries, for she has lost her majestic charm,

She has lost her composure,
She no longer is a place of refuge
She bears untold secrets, and her breathtaking horizon repulses
her maker,
Her sobs and weeping are deafening to the ear

The stately and majestic mountain,
Whose horizon once excited the beholder's eye
Now cries for she has become haunted
Her cries; even she can no longer bear

The morning song she no longer sings,
Hers is not a melodious tune
Instead she cries bitterly,
The mountain cries

Behind the Inspiration

Life can be, and at the best of times, is such a blur and so
confusing. Which one of us can say they truly understand life?
What appears to be a place of refuge sometimes turns and can
be what hurts us.

A Better Half of Humanity

She was beautiful.
She was kindness itself.
She was a woman.
She fell in love.
Alas it was forbidden love!

Six months to go, she would have rocked the cradle
Sending her little one to a peaceful slumber.
Six more months, and her maternal instincts would have come
to fruition.
Six months, the baby would have sucked from her tender,
loving breasts.
Hers was a forbidden kind of love.

Happy to have found the one
The man she truly loved
The man her heart chose.
Only him she vowed to love forever
Her soul connected with his.

Was she not a better half of humanity?

What was her crime?

Her crime they say was to fall in love with the man she so dearly loved.

Her crime they say was to be a woman of their culture.

When did she cease to be Daddy's best girl?

Or rather, was she ever Daddy's girl?

Did he not have dreams over her daughter?

The one she looked up to for protection

The man she was proud to show off and call Daddy

The man she saw as the unconquerable

The hero her eyes first beheld

Became the first to cast the stone

The stone that lead to her brutal death.

Was she not a better half of humanity?

Her crime was to fall in love.

Her crime was to defy culture.

Her crime was her quest to be a unique, independent and intelligent woman.

Is she not a better half of humanity?

Because she follows her heart.

Stoned to death, not by strangers

But by the men who should have lain down their lives for her.

They looked her in the eye
As they carried out the evil deed.
She was a better half of humanity

She was beautiful, she was kind
She was strong
She was a mother-to-be.

They call it honour killing.
What honour is in killing another?
Shame on those that took her life
For she stood for her right
The right to love the one she chose
Indeed she was a true better half to humanity.

To all the women that have surpassed us.
To all the women shackled by barbaric inhumane beliefs.
Whose lives are brutally snuffed out.
We vow today and always
The fight will continue
Every girl, every woman
A better half of humanity.

Behind the Inspiration

In memory of Farzana Parveen. One of many women killed in the barbaric guise of 'honour killing'.

Only I

Only I can know, only I can tell
For only I have worn the shoes; and only I know how they fit
For that I deserve your accolade

Only I know the pain of mistakes made, only I know the grief
that loss brings
Only I know how long and lonely the night can be
For only I have experienced loss and meditated with tears in the
night
For that I deserve your respect

Only I know the turmoil of separation from loved ones, the guilt
it brings
For only I have lived it
For that you should not be judge and jury
For if the shoe was on your foot, would you dare to take the
walk?

Only I know the misery rejection brings, for only I have been rejected

Only I have mastered the art to look back at the roads once trodden

Dismiss bitterness and beam with an electrifying smile

Only I know how to laugh as I kick off the many different shoes and wait for the next pair

The journey is incomplete; many a pair of different shoes still await my battered feet

For that I deserve your accolade

For only I

<u>Behind the Inspiration</u>

Until you have worn the shoes that life's challenges have dealt another woman you do not have the right to be judge and jury. Unless you have trodden the road that another has, never trivialise their feelings and experiences, instead learn life's great lessons from such.

Somehow

The early birds chime a melodious tune
She tosses and turns in her bed as one who is annoyed
The birds greet the morn with song and anticipation
Somehow she dreads the breaking of the new day

The wind echoes the sound of the morn, ruffling the sleepy leaves
Bringing them into full arousal, and soon all will be light
She stirs and slowly stretches to conjure life into her lifeless body
Reluctant to greet the new day

Somehow she dreads the uncertainty this day brings;
The day reminds her of faded dreams, the misery of the heart
And yet she must wade through it

She stares through the window, eyes full of fear
Will this day somehow be different?
Without an answer she wonders

How the wind, the rustling leaves and the singing birds excite at
the dawning day
Wishing the elements could answer her, she must get through
the somewhat bleak day

The street is suddenly abuzz with excited children;
Excited and full of anticipation at the breaking of a new day
She watches their innocent faces, oblivious of her dilemma
Somehow she must dig deep inside and find strength for the day

She laments within herself; the day has finally dawned
The night's weeping soon must cease for it's a new day, a new
beginning
Somehow she must get by
Not so sure how, but she knows she must face today
Somehow she will overcome, she will make it through

Out of nothing she appears to have created a somewhat edible
meal
I can assure you it was not a magic trick!
She has learnt to survive
Smiling as she gazes upon her brood partaking of the portions
Somehow she appears to have made it

As dusk gently knocks, she looks back and wonders how she made it through the day

With courage, she made it through another bloodsucking day

And yet she still has a bit of life left in her

With a faint pulse still felt, she will wake again in the morrow and somehow swim through the life-sucking day

Somehow she must survive; for to others she is the gift that has to keep on giving

<u>Behind the Inspiration</u>

'When the rubber meets the road,' and all is crumbling around you. When you don't have an answer or solution, what do you do? Do you throw your hands in the air and give up? Somehow you have to learn to survive through that day.

Woman

When I am weak, then I realise how strong I am
When I cry then I realise I am really strong.
My tears don't spell weakness, they mean strength
A strong woman cries

My silence does not mean victim, but spells survivor
You boast you have broken me yet you have made me stronger
The soul you once raptured is now the strongest
The soul you once fractured is now mended
I am a woman; a strong woman

I pity you for you will never know my strength
Many a mile the journey to recovery takes
Rest assured the journey will be complete
For I am a woman; a very strong woman

Steep mountains I will have to climb
Many rivers I might have to cross
Rest assured the journey will be complete
I am a woman; a strong woman

<u>Behind the Inspiration</u>

I make no apologies for all the strong women; some misjudged and others greatly misunderstood. Don't just be a woman, be a strong one. It's not about your physicality but your ability.

Mother

Yes she is a woman
A simple woman
And she is my mother

She is the reason I am.
The reason I have become who I am
She is my mother

She taught me how to be a woman,
Not just a woman
But a strong, self-sufficient woman

She taught me to be a good mother
I hope I have been so.
Let my children live to tell the tale.

She is full of wisdom
Her knowledge is priceless
Her love, selfless
Her strength, fearless

Her aura exudes warmth
She taught me to be a woman
She holds no degree
No PhD attached to her name
Her qualities, precious stones
Rare and hard to find

She is my mother
A confidante when I've been confused
A loving disciplinarian when I strayed
My failures, she turned into precious life lessons

She wiped tears when I cried
Shared soothing words when I was in distress
My faults, she magnified them not
She is the woman that is my mother

No degree, no PhD attached to her name
Who dares tell me she falls short?
Tell me she has no letters attached to her name?
She is the woman that made me
Gems of her knowledge are priceless
Her wisdom is all I needed
I will forever cherish her until I breathe my last.
Mum you are a gem, I will always love you

<u>*Behind the Inspiration*</u>

Mothers still need their mothers. I reflected on the precious woman who is my mother. She is the whole reason I am the woman I am today and beyond. You also have something to say to your mum. Say it now!

Motherhood

'Your suspicions are real!'
The good-looking doc smiled at her
'A little life is indeed growing inside of you.'
A life for her to nurture and care for

She became big and funny shaped
An old friend told her she looked gorgeous
'Shaped that way?' She giggled
How she was shaped meant nothing
You! Inside of her was all that mattered
That little life in her

Left, right and centre poured in advice on her impending
motherhood
Great and silly advice, those were not in short supply
As the months wasted away
She wondered about this little life

The first time she held you in her arms, her tears welcomed you
They streaked down the puffy cheeks
How she had laboured for this little life to be in the world
Hers were tears of joy
For this life now in her hands
For her to nurture and love

'Hello little one. This is your mummy.'
She whispered into your little wrinkly ears
She promised to love and take care of you
A bystander laughed and mocked,
'The child can't hear you.'
She made fun of that sacred moment
A moment between mother and child

This little life, entrusted to her, a mere mortal
This little life for her to love, nurture and lay down her own life
for
Nine months of cravings, cramps and cracked heels
Brings forth the life of a child
A life she vows to nurture and protect

She held on to you and admired your peaceful innocent face
Now a mother, she embraces this gift of motherhood
'I will care and protect you with my whole being,' she vows
This little life will now call me mother
I am blessed to be gifted with motherhood
Your little life is for me to nurture and love.

<u>*Behind the Inspiration*</u>

To all those women that have nurtured and loved a helpless baby/child I celebrate you and may you forever be honoured. Had you not embraced this special gift of motherhood, many a child would have lost out on life.

Fruits of my Womb

They come into our lives and give us a purpose.
Helpless little babes in our arms
We nurse, nurture and care for; these the fruits of our wombs

Soon they grow into their own selves; become their own persons
It scares us to watch them develop into big people; soon a young lady; soon a young man.
These the fruits of our wombs

Our lives are filled with the joy they bring
We are blessed to be part of your lives; to share those intimate moments
And to pass down family traditions.

To our little princesses; now beautiful young ladies, preserve your identity
Depend not; be dependable
Be strong women, the best you can be
Let wisdom and kindness be your covering
You the fruits of our womb

To our little princes; now fine young men
Be men of integrity; men that are true to their word
Be the best you can be; be strong, be accountable
You the fruits of our womb

Both fulfil your promises
Bring healing and comfort to those around you
Be the best there ever will be
That's what the world needs
You; the fruits of our womb

To some you are the fruits of the heart
For our wombs are closed, not cursed as others tend to think
Through our hearts we bore you
You are the fruits of our hearts
With closed wombs, we also boast for the fruits we have loved,
nurtured and cared for
These the fruits of our souls and our wombs

Behind the Inspiration

To every child that has been born, fostered or adopted; you are very special. To every female that has cared for and nurtured a child this is for you. A special thanks to my own sister. She is a one in a million.

The Small Suitcase

The flight had to be swift and smooth, every second was crucial
The journey sudden and urgent!
A small suitcase had to suffice.

A small suitcase with all that mattered.
A small suitcase to hold my belongings to a country of safety
A small suitcase defined me.

Other travellers wheel expensive suitcases full of fripperies.
Mine a small suitcase and yet holding all of me

My small suitcase light as a feather; and yet held all of me!
I trusted the contents of my small suitcase to sustain me.
The small suitcase was all I had; the small suitcase contained all
that really mattered.
All that mattered was in the small suitcase.

What's with the small suitcase you ask?
The small suitcase you see is all of me, I try to explain.
All that I really need for now is inside.

A pair of black shoes a must for every woman.
Two decent reasonable long skirts in case I need to dress up.
Two packets of sanitary towels to preserve 'that time of the month'.
One coat to provide warmth.
A pair of jeans to cover my weary legs.
Photographs of my nearest and dearest, to force a smile on dark, lonely days
The Bible, to find comfort when in distress, to keep wide open next to me in the dead of the night *
The small suitcase contained all of me.
The small handheld suitcase and yet priceless.

*A tradition passed on to me by my grandmother when I first left home to teach in the rural areas believed to be plagued with evil spirits

Behind the Inspiration

When the urgent need to survive is all that matters, possessions cease to matter. This depicts a journey to safety once undertaken.

Hope

Define it to me
What colour is it?
And what shape is it?

At night she lies in the dark
Despair is in her face
Hopelessness, the song in the night

Tell me, what colour is hope?
What shape does it resemble?
For when I lay me down to sleep
I'm filled with dread and despair

A girlfriend came along
She dared to unwrap hope
So tell me what colour is hope?
I dared to ask

'The colour of hope I might not know
'It's shape I might not define
'It's characteristics I might not fully grasp
'What I know is, I embraced hope'

With attentive ears I paid attention
As she tried to win me over to her hope side
Feeling somewhat short changed
'So tell me what colour is hope?'
Only this time my question was mocking her

Like a child who has lost her way home in a thick forest
She held my hand and took me down memory lane
Not that I had forgotten
But I needed reminding

As a mother soothing her little one she took me down the
memory lane of her life
I remembered, hope is what she hung on to when all seemed
hopeless
She reminded me of words of hope I had shared with her
'So tell me what colour is hope?
This time she asked me

Hope has no colour, shape or form
Hope is the feeling not to give up
When life goes belly up
Hope is not knowing what tomorrow will be
But having the conviction, it will be all right

'Do you still ask the question?'
'No,' I answered with a smile
Hope is allowing a dream to occupy your mind when another
has faded
Hope produces results

We hugged and kissed
With hands intertwined
We walked into hopeland
And hoped all will be as all should be

<u>*Behind the Inspiration*</u>

*Hope urges us to get on. It has no face and no form and yet it's so
powerful it can change our perspective on the unknown future.*

Connecting Souls

The man-made bird scales the skies and flies into the highest
heavens
I sit, one whose soul is torn apart
Deep in thought I wonder if souls will once again cleave and
cling

Emotions marvel at keeping me a prisoner
Angry, Scared, Happy, Sad, I let them conquer
How I wish just one of them could be my master
You see, one, I'm sure I can handle
I try and console my aching heart
Joy! Where on earth are you?
Drive these away and possess me

The years have swiftly rolled by
Deliberately I stopped counting
Memories of home, a happy innocent childhood
My first kiss, my first class award and friends of old
They all are but a distant memory.

When I behold the yellow ribbon, will souls reconnect?
That yellow ribbon, signalling home sweet home
Will I connect; will home sweet home connect with me?
Swiftly gone by: the years have ripped me of a soul
Is my soul willing to connect with home?

The big bird cruises the skies, thousands of air miles it covers
Time ticks by, and still the emotions hold me a prisoner
I am scared to my wits' end
Scared to behold an ageing mum
Petrified at the thought of an ailing father
How I want our souls to automatically reconnect

The old oak tree is not in sight to tie the yellow ribbon
This time the yellow ribbon is in its rightful place
Tied on the hearts of those I have longed for.
You see that's all I need.

They say, 'Home is where the heart is'
Why am I so overtaken by emotions?
Please heart; reconnect with the souls of those I have longed for

The bird lands, it's such a smooth land I feel not a thud
The walk from the big bird to waiting fields of people is indeed
the 'long walk home'
Instantly eyes search for loved ones, my loved ones
Eyes meet!
Suddenly paralysis hits me. I attempt a scream only to realise
I've been slapped by muteism
The language of tears says it all
Connect as we connect, what was now isn't
I behold my loved ones
The rest is a blur
When I finally open my eyes, souls have connected

Regina Jele-Ncube

<u>Behind the Inspiration</u>

There are times when what should otherwise be normal and straightforward is really not so. Joyous occasions can cause us anxiety and untold fear that we cannot explain because we don't understand ourselves. A journey that had to be taken to reconnect with loved ones had its toll on me. Everyone around me expected me to be over the moon. This is dedicated to the memory of my beloved dad who passed away before the journey was taken. Make your goodbyes count. That goodbye you say today could really be the final one. Rest a little while 'mdala Jele'.

Give me my Flowers

Violets, lilies and roses
They covered the big auditorium, allowing different scents to fill
the room
Much to the delight of the waiting crowd
Indulging their sense of smell to their hearts' content

The auditorium, filled up with those that loved her and knew
her.
Those she once loved, those she once nursed
They each carried flowers; a mark of their love

I looked on and admired the adorned room,
Now turned into a garden of glorious sweet-smelling flowers,
How I wished she could also admire them,
How I wished she could sniff their sweet aroma

I looked on and wondered,
Had this crowd ever given her flowers while she walked
amongst them?

Had this crowd ever given her flowers when she still had breath
to smell them?
Had this crowd given her flowers to cheer her up on those
gloomy days?
Had they ever given her flowers at all?

I looked on and wondered
Had this crowd given her flowers to say I love you?
Had any of them given her flowers to show how much they
appreciated her?
Had any of them ever given her the time of day?
Had any ever told her how much she meant?

Then I remembered those that I love,
And vowed to give them flowers while they can appreciate them
To give them flowers while they can still see them

I vowed,
To give them flowers when they can still smell them,
To give them flowers when they can bring a glowing radiance to
their faces
I vowed,
To take time out for those that I love while they still have breath

Behind the Inspiration
_____

A funeral once attended had all the 'trappings and trimmings' of sickening luxury. I really wondered if the 'living' had lavished the 'deceased' while they were still alive and able to appreciate all this.

Love Me

Your touch sends shivers down my spine
My heart melts like chocolate subjected to soaring temperatures.
At the mention of your name I almost lose my senses and my
mind deserts me
You are the love of my life

No other gives me pleasure as you do
Your gentle touch, your soft whispers tickle my spine
You, only are the love of my life

Many suitors craved for my love;
 You came along and stole my heart
You ran with it to heights unimaginable
My heart intertwined with yours

Will you love me for me?
Will you forsake all others who crave your love?
Will your heart love only me?
Do you swear to love me for me?

Out of many souls, I chose yours
I gave you the gift of my love
From my heart to yours
I promise to be yours forever

Will you also love me for me?
Do you promise to have and to hold only me and no other?
Will you walk by my side and catch me when I fall?
I love you for you; can you love me for me?

<u>Behind the Inspiration</u>

Every one of us is a sociable being and needs to be loved. Can we truly love someone for who they are?

Regina Jele-Ncube

About the Author:

Regina Ncube (nee Jele) was born in Zimbabwe, Bulawayo. She describes herself firstly as a woman, a daughter and a mother. She sees herself as a feminist who realises she cannot personally solve issues affecting women but seeking to make a huge difference in the immediate spheres of her influence. Surrounded by and brought up by a strong woman, she salutes all the women that have made an impact and made a difference. She has a few writing projects up her sleeve.

Regina Jele-Ncube

About the Compilation

Deep Within My Soul, a compilation of fourteen poems, thoughts, expressions and feelings based on the many experiences in the life of a woman. She looks deep within her soul and digs out that which matters most. She realises she has been 'just scratching the surface'. As she embarks on this soul-searching journey, she is amazed at what is unearthed. Deep within her soul she finds a sea of unspoken words; words of adoration and pride to the entire sisterhood. She affirms the strong woman; to penning words in praise of her own mother. She celebrates the gift of love extended by intriguing women who have opened their hearts and loved a child regardless of whether they are biologically linked or not. Deep within each of our souls lays the mystery of who we really are.

Lightning Source UK Ltd.
Milton Keynes UK
UKOW04f1658141015

260525UK00001B/2/P